W9-CAG-737

Music & Movement
IN THE
Classroom

Grades PreK–K

WRITTEN BY Steven Traugh

Featuring the songs of Youngheart Music's
Greg Scelsa and Steve Millang

EDITOR Cindy Truitt

ILLUSTRATOR Catherine Rader

COVER PHOTOGRAPHER Michael Jarrett

DESIGNER Moonhee Pak

COVER DESIGNER Moonhee Pak

ART DIRECTOR Tom Cochrane

PROJECT DIRECTOR Carolea Williams

Table of Contents

INTRODUCTION 4

LESSON **1** CAN'T SIT STILL 6
Listening and following directions

LESSON **2** GOOD MORNING 8
Learning to add steady beat movements to a song

LESSON **3** WHAT COLORS DID YOU CHOOSE? 10
Recognizing colors in clothing

LESSON **4** MIXING MY COLORS 12
Mixing primary colors to make secondary colors

LESSON **5** MACK CHICKEN DANCE MEDLEY 14
Learning to do movements to music

LESSON **6** DINOSAURS DANCING 16
Counting up to seven

LESSON **7** HALLOWEEN ON PARADE 18
Learning to march to a steady beat

LESSON **8** BODY TALK 20
Introduction to singing with an echo game

LESSON **9** SHAPING UP WITH SHAPES 22
Recognizing shapes

LESSON **10** ACROSS THE BRIDGE 24
Learning to walk in a line as a class

LESSON **11** COUNTING UP TO TWENTY 26
Counting forward up to twenty in a song

LESSON **12** ALPHABET SOUP 28
Learning the alphabet through a song

LESSON **13** BINGO 30
Clapping a rhythm pattern that grows in length

LESSON **14** THE NAME CLAPPING GAME 32
Clapping to the letters in a name

LESSON **15** NEW ZOO REVIEW 34
Creating animal movements to music

LESSON **16**   WARMIN' UP. 36
Listening to music and executing movements

LESSON **17**   DAYS OF THE WEEK. 38
Learning the days of the week in English and Spanish

LESSON **18**   ROCK 'ROUND THE MULBERRY BUSH. 40
Promoting good personal hygiene

LESSON **19**   WHAT WILL WE DO WHEN WE ALL GO OUT TO PLAY? . . 42
Improving language arts skills

LESSON **20**   LISTEN AND MOVE. 44
Listening and moving to music

LESSON **21**   QUIET TIME 46
Moving in slow motion

LESSON **22**   A-HUNTING WE WILL GO 47
Creating movements to dramatize a song

LESSON **23**   THE BEANBAG BOOGIE 49
Balancing a beanbag in various ways

LESSON **24**   SKIP TO MY LOO 51
Creating movements described in a song

LESSON **25**   RIDING IN MY CAR 53
Comparing and contrasting steps to riding in a car

LESSON **26**   BODY PART MOVEMENT MARCH 55
Learning steady beat movements

LESSON **27**   READING RHYTHMIC NOTATION #1. 57
Reading quarter notes and rests in music

LESSON **28**   READING RHYTHMIC NOTATION #2. 58
Improving reading quarter notes and rests in music

LESSON **29**   THE HOKEY POKEY. 59
Learning left and right

LESSON **30**   SNOWFLAKE. 61
Exploring uniqueness

Introduction

Music & Movement in the Classroom is a complete program of materials and teaching techniques designed to channel children's natural enthusiasm for music and movement into productive learning experiences. Designed for the elementary teacher, this program features clear step-by-step lesson plans along with exciting and engaging songs and stories that make teaching enjoyable for the musical novice and expert alike.

The program outlined in this book is easy to integrate into your weekly lesson plans. The 30-lesson developmental curriculum provides one 20–25 minute lesson per week. Each lesson introduces a new song and movement activity, to be followed by a 20–25 minute review that same week.

Each lesson reinforces the skill and content taught in reading, writing, social studies, and science. Counting, sequencing, and pattern recognition become meaningful to children in lessons that use the relationship between rhythm and math. Singing activities use the lyrics of songs to enhance vocabulary, oral expression, and reading.

Use this program to meet the needs of each child. By offering a wide variety of experiences that include listening and moving, these lessons allow you to teach to the children's strongest learning modalities. Lessons have a profound impact, which results in a longer attention span and greater retention.

The activities in *Music & Movement in the Classroom* encourage self-expression. The performance activities offer opportunities for children to use their own creativity and to work with others. They see their own potential and growth in self-esteem, as well as in their appreciation of each other.

How to Use These Materials

This curriculum lends itself to many classroom applications. The presentation and structure of the materials in this book and on the CDs have been designed for the teacher who finds music and movement to be new or unfamiliar areas of the curriculum. The 30 lessons are presented in a developmental progression that has been proven effective in a wide variety of prekindergarten and kindergarten settings. However, for the teacher who already uses music and movement in the classroom, the order and content of the materials can be altered and adapted to supplement the existing program.

Each activity page includes objectives and skills reinforced in the lesson. In preparation for most lessons, you may want to make a transparency of the lyric page to display on an overhead projecter for children to see. Give a copy of each lyric page to children to color and keep in a folder. Or, enlarge a copy of each lyric page, decorate it, and display it on a bulletin board.

This curriculum is designed for the needs and abilities of a wide variety of prekindergarten and kindergarten students. You are encouraged to adapt these materials to meet the needs of your class. Students need not have received Music & Movement in the Classroom instruction at previous grade levels in order to be successful with the activities presented in any successive grade level.

The Lessons

1. Schedule 20 to 25 minutes of instruction at a regular time twice a week (a total of 40 to 50 minutes of weekly instruction). Introduce each lesson on the first day of weekly music instruction, and reinforce it on a second day that same week.

2. The lessons generally fall into one of three categories:
   - movement activities
   - singing activities
   - rhythmic activities

   Lessons in all three areas progress from easy introductory activities to more challenging applications. Successive lessons vary in the type of activity.

3. Each lesson should be done with a review of the previous lesson's activity. This is done for two reasons:
   - Students increase their level of performance with the additional participation that a review provides.
   - The main activity of the lesson combined with the review activity allows students to participate in a variety of activities each week.

4. Begin each lesson with a vocal warm-up. Have the class warm up their voices by making a sliding sound that moves from a low pitch to a high pitch and back to a low pitch again—like a siren. Do this several times, reminding children not to yell.

Scheduling

The typical school year contains 36 to 38 weeks of instruction. At the rate of one lesson per week, this curriculum requires 30 weeks to complete. The lessons in this curriculum are divided into two sections. Each section contains fifteen lessons. Teachers with traditional schedules should plan to complete Lessons 1 through 15 the first semester and Lessons 16 through 30 the second semester. Teachers on year-round tracks should plan to complete approximately eight lessons for each of the nine-week sessions. (Other year-round configurations will require adjustments to this schedule.)

The Compact Discs

Two CDs are included with the book for this curriculum. The CDs contain all the music used in the lessons. Each activity page lists the music and track number(s) for that lesson.

1

Can't Sit Still

Objectives

♪ To introduce body movement to music

♪ To promote the ability to listen to directions and execute tasks

♪ To improve coordination

Skills

♪ Listening

♪ Movement

♪ Coordination

Music

CD #1, Track 1: "Can't Sit Still"

ACTIVITY

1 Have children stand facing you. Have them stand at least an arm's length apart from each other in all directions.

2 Tell the class that they are about to hear some music. Tell children to listen to the music carefully because they will be following the directions given in the song.

3 Play the song "Can't Sit Still," and have the class move with you as you model the movements described in the song to the beat of the music. Repeat as desired.

4 Have volunteers lead the rest of the class in performing the movements. Have new leaders repeat the activity.

EXTENSION

Have children sit in a circle and discuss the title "Can't Sit Still." Ask if there is a time that sitting still is necessary. Help them to name appropriate times to sit still in class (e.g., circle time, reading time, listening time). Have each child draw a picture of a time when it is necessary to sit still. Collect all the papers, and use them to create a list of classroom rules regarding sitting still. A sample rule might be "I will sit still and listen to my teacher when she is giving us directions." Write a rule at the bottom of each paper, and bind the papers into a book titled *We Can Sit Still*. Encourage children to read and review these classroom rules throughout the school year.

Can't Sit Still

Words and Music by Greg Scelsa
Copyright 1995, Gregorian Chance Music (ASCAP)

Spoken:
Well, if you can't sit still,
Here's a game we play.
Listen to the words and do what we say.

I've got my fingers wigglin' to the rhythm,
I've got my fingers wigglin' to the rhythm,
I've got my fingers wigglin' to the rhythm,
And I can't sit still.

I've got my shoulders wigglin' to the rhythm,
I've got my shoulders wigglin' to the rhythm,
I've got my shoulders wigglin' to the rhythm,
And I can't sit still.

I've got my nose wigglin' to the rhythm,
I've got my nose wigglin' to the rhythm,
I've got my nose wigglin' to the rhythm,
And I can't sit still.

I've got my knees wigglin' to the rhythm,
I've got my knees wigglin' to the rhythm,
I've got my knees wigglin' to the rhythm,
And I can't sit still.

I've got my chin wigglin' to the rhythm,
I've got my chin wigglin' to the rhythm,
I've got my chin wigglin' to the rhythm,
And I can't sit still.

Spoken:
Now touch your head,
Touch your shoulders,
Touch your knees,
Now your toes.
Touch your shoulders,
Now your toes.
Touch your knees,
Now your head.
Listen now! Head, shoulders, knees, and
toes!
Touch your shoulders, knees,
Now your toes.
Touch your head,
Shake your body all about,

Now everybody freeze.

I've got my head shakin' to the rhythm,
I've got my head shakin' to the rhythm,
I've got my head shakin' to the rhythm,
And I can't sit still.

I've got my toes wigglin' to the rhythm,
I've got my toes wigglin' to the rhythm,
I've got my toes wigglin' to the rhythm,
And I can't sit still.

I've got my elbows wigglin' to the rhythm,
I've got my elbows wigglin' to the rhythm,
I've got my elbows wigglin' to the rhythm,
And I can't sit still.

I've got my hands clappin' to the rhythm,
I've got my hands clappin' to the rhythm,
I've got my hands clappin' to the rhythm,
And I can't sit still.

No, I can't, I can't sit still.

2

Good Morning

Objectives

♪ To sing the song "Good Morning"

♪ To add steady beat movements to the song

Skills

♪ Singing

♪ Movement

♪ Expression

♪ Rhythm

Music

CD #1, Track 2: "Good Morning"

ACTIVITY

1 Have children sit in a circle. Read the lyrics of the song "Good Morning" to the class one line at a time while doing the corresponding movement. Have children echo the words and movements in response.

2 Play "Good Morning," and lead your class in the movements as they listen to the lyrics. Encourage children to tap a steady beat on their legs during the instrumental interlude in the middle of the song.

3 Play "Good Morning" again, and lead the class in singing and moving to the music. Repeat as desired.

4 Remind the class to smile when they sing, as some children tend to yell instead of sing when they get excited. It's almost impossible to smile and yell at the same time.

EXTENSION

Help children create other steady beat movements to do during the instrumental interlude. Ask for suggestions. Select children who wish to lead the class in moving to "Good Morning" and the instrumental interlude. Have new leaders repeat the activity.

Good Morning

Words and Music by Bill Fletcher
Copyright 1978, Little House Music (ASCAP)

Good morning.	*(wave left hand)*
Good morning.	*(wave right hand)*
Good morning to you!	*(wave both hands and then point at the class on the word "you")*
Good morning.	*(wave left hand)*
Good morning.	*(wave right hand)*
Good morning to you!	*(wave both hands and then point at the class on the word "you")*
Our day is beginning.	*(sweep hands upward from waist, palms out, moving hands apart as they ascend)*
There's so much to do.	*(cup chin in hands and purse lips)*
Good morning.	*(wave left hand)*
Good morning.	*(wave right hand)*
Good morning to you!	*(wave both hands and then point at the class on the word "you")*

Instrumental Interlude

(Repeat from beginning)

3

What Colors Did You Choose?

Objectives

♪ To recognize colors in clothing

♪ To improve singing skills

Skills

♪ Listening

♪ Singing

♪ Rhythm

♪ Movement

♪ Color Recognition

Music

CD #1, Track 3:
"What Colors
Did You Choose?"

ACTIVITY

1 Have children sit in a circle. Tell the class that they are about to play a game that will help them look for different colors in their clothes. Invite a child who is wearing red to sit in the front of the class and be the leader. Play the song "What Colors Did You Choose?" During the first verse, have the child lead all the others wearing red to stand and point to the color red on their clothes.

2 Pause the CD. Choose a child who is wearing blue to be the leader for the next section, and then continue the song.

3 Continue to choose new leaders for the other colors in the song.

4 Repeat the activity, and encourage the class to sing along with the children's voices on the CD. Repeat as desired.

EXTENSION

Paint each of six boxes one color from the song. Label each box with the appropriate color word. Have children place objects from the classroom or home in the corresponding color boxes. Display each set of items. Point out the different shades, hues, and intensities of a given color.

What Colors Did You Choose?

Words and Music by Steven Traugh. Copyright 1988, Kiducation

Red, red, can you see red?
Yes, yes, we can see red.
Red, red, tomatoes are red?
Yes, yes, tomatoes are red.
Tomatoes are red just like you said.

Chorus:
  Hey, look at your clothes. What colors did
    you choose?
  Pants and shirts and socks and shoes.
  If you're wearing (red), it's time to stand
  And point to the color with a finger or a hand.

Blue, blue, can you see blue?
Yes, yes, we can see blue.
Blue, blue, the sky is blue?
Yes, yes, the sky is blue.
The sky is blue. It's true. It's true.
(Chorus)

Green, green, can you see green?
Yes, yes, we can see green.
Green, green, the grass is green?
Yes, yes, the grass is green.
The greenest grass that we have ever seen.
(Chorus)

Yellow, yellow, can you see yellow?
Yes, yes, we can see yellow.
Yellow, yellow, bananas are yellow?
Yes, yes, bananas are yellow.
Take some bananas and make some yellow Jell-O.
(Chorus)

Orange, orange, can you see orange?
Yes, yes, we can see orange.
Orange, orange, bananas are orange?
No, no, bananas aren't orange.
Bananas are yellow, but pumpkins
  are orange.
(Chorus)

Purple, purple, can you see purple?
Yes, yes, we can see purple.
Purple, purple, is grape juice purple?
Yes, yes, grape juice is purple.
Grape juice is purple and sweet as maple surple.
(Chorus)

Spoken:
*Now let's hear if you remember the colors of all
the things we named in the song. I'll say the name
three times and then you say the color.*

Tomatoes, tomatoes, tomatoes are (red).
Did you say "red"? (Yes!)
The sky, the sky, the sky is (blue).
Did you say "blue"? (Yes!)
The grass, the grass, the grass is (green).
Did you say "green"? (Yes!)
Bananas, bananas, bananas are (yellow).
Did you say "yellow"? (Yes!)
Pumpkins, pumpkins, pumpkins are (orange).
Did you say "orange"? (Yes!)
Grape juice, grape juice, grape juice is (purple).
Did you say "purple"? (Yes!)

Now faster!
Tomatoes are (red).
The sky is (blue).
The grass is (green).
Pumpkins are (orange).
Grape juice is (purple).

Hey, look at your clothes. What colors did
  you choose?
Pants and shirts and socks and shoes.
Look at your teacher and raise your hand.
Then tell of all the colors that you're wearing
  if you can.

Mixing My Colors

Objectives

♪ To learn how primary colors blend to make secondary colors

♪ To improve singing skills

Skills

♪ Singing

♪ Color Recognition

Music

CD #1, Track 4: "Mixing My Colors"

ACTIVITY

1 In advance, collect paints, crayons, markers, or color transparencies to use in a demonstration to show what happens when you mix primary colors.

2 Demonstrate how to mix the three primary colors—red, blue, and yellow—in pairs to create three secondary colors as follows:

red and blue = purple
blue and yellow = green
yellow and red = orange

3 Play the song "Mixing My Colors," and repeat your demonstration in time with the music as children listen to the song.

4 Play the song again. Ask children to concentrate on the game in the second part of the song. Have them point to an example of a secondary color as they fill in the correct color word in time with the music. Repeat as desired.

EXTENSION

Have the class use finger paints to mix primary colors to make secondary colors. Present only two primary colors at one time as it is tempting to mix all three together at once. Have each child use these new colors to create pictures of pumpkins, grass, and grapes to use with "Mixing My Colors." Have children sing along with the song and hold up the appropriate pictures in time with the lyrics.

Mixing My Colors

Words and Music by Steven Traugh
Copyright 1990, Kiducation (ASCAP)

Well, I'm mixing my colors just for fun.
You know red and blue and yellow are the ones.
With just red and blue and yellow
I'll make purple, orange, and green.
Yes, I'll make the prettiest colors ever seen.

Well, I'm mixing red and yellow to make orange.
Yes, I'm mixing red and yellow to make orange.
I'll make pumpkins just for fun,
When all my mixing's done,
Just like orange pumpkins growing in the sun.

Well, I'm mixing blue and yellow to make green.
Yes, I'm mixing blue and yellow to make green.
I'll make green grass just for fun,
When all my mixing's done,
Just like green grass growing in the sun.

Well, I'm mixing red and blue to make purple.
Yes, I'm mixing red and blue to make purple.
I'll make purple grapes just for fun,
When all my mixing's done,
Just like purple grapes growing in the sun.

5

Mack Chicken Dance Medley

Objectives

♪ To listen for a steady beat in music

♪ To follow a four-step movement pattern to a steady beat

♪ To listen and follow directions in music

♪ To follow tempo changes

♪ To improve coordination skills

Skills

♪ Listening

♪ Patterning

♪ Coordination

♪ Concentration

♪ Movement

Music

CD #1, Track 5: "Mack Chicken Dance Medley"

ACTIVITY

1 Have children face you and stand at least one arm's length from each other in all directions.

2 Teach the class the following movements to the "Chicken Dance":
- Form both hands into a hen's beak at shoulder height with four fingers opposing the thumb to create a chicken mouth opening and closing. Do this movement quickly four times to the beat of the music. Beak-beak-beak-beak.
- Put both hands under your armpits to form chicken wings. Flap your wings quickly four times to the beat of the music. Flap-flap-flap-flap.
- With your hands still under your arms wave your "tail feathers" quickly four times to the beat of the music. Tail-tail-tail-tail.
- Clap quickly four times to the beat of the music. (You can hear the claps in the music.)

3 Have children practice the movements slowly, and then pick up the tempo until it coincides with the beat of the music.

4 For the second part of the "Chicken Dance," have children pair up, lock arms, and turn in a circle four times.

5 Review with the class the movements to "Itsy Bitsy Spider" and "Head, Shoulders, Knees, and Toes."

6 Play the song "Mack Chicken Dance Medley," and lead the class in performing the movements in time with the music. Repeat as desired.

EXTENSION

Select children who wish to lead the class in moving to "Mack Chicken Dance Medley." Have new leaders repeat the activity.

Mack Chicken Dance Medley

The Chicken Dance, Copyright September Music (ASCAP)
Itsy Bitsy Spider, Copyright Kazoo/Little House Music (ASCAP)
Head, Shoulders, Knees & Toes, Copyright Kazoo Music/Little House Music (ASCAP)

Part A:
The Chicken Dance Instrumental

Part B:
Itsy Bitsy Spider

The itsy bitsy spider
Went up the water spout.
Down came the rain
And washed the spider out.
Out came the sun
And dried up all the rain,
And the itsy bitsy spider
Went up the spout again.

(Repeat)

Part C:
Head, Shoulders, Knees, & Toes

Head and shoulders, knees and toes,
  knees and toes
Head and shoulders, knees and toes,
  knees and toes
Eyes and ears and mouth and nose
Head and shoulders, knees and toes

(Repeat)

6

Dinosaurs Dancing

Objectives

♪ To improve counting skills and number concepts

♪ To strengthen singing skills

♪ To develop movement skills to coordinate with music

Skills

♪ Counting

♪ Creativity

♪ Singing

Music

CD #1, Track 6: "Dinosaurs Dancing"

ACTIVITY

1 In advance, create movements for the song "Dinosaurs Dancing." Before you introduce movements to the class, practice them until you are proficient.

2 Have children face you and stand at least one arm's length away from each other in all directions.

3 Play "Dinosaurs Dancing," and lead children in performing the movements in time with the music. Repeat as desired. Encourage children to sing along with the music while they do the movements.

4 Have several children lead the class in moving and singing with the music. Ask for new volunteers to repeat the activity.

EXTENSIONS

• Have children draw pictures that illustrate the song lyrics.

• Have the class create lines for 8, 9, and 10. Have children create movements and illustrations for the new lyrics.

• Include this lesson in a larger unit on the study of dinosaurs.

Dinosaurs Dancing

Words by Luella Connelly. Music by Steven Traugh
Copyright 1991, Kiducation (ASCAP)

Di–dino–dinosaurs dancing.
Dinosaurs dancing I see 1.
Dinosaurs dance.
Dance, dance, dancing.
Dinosaurs dancing in the noonday sun.
La, la, la, la 1.
Dinosaurs dancing in the noonday sun.

Di–dino–dinosaurs dancing.
Dinosaurs dancing I see 2.
Dinosaurs dance.
Dance, dance, dancing.
Dinosaurs dancing in the morning dew.
La, la, la, la 1.
La, la, la, la 2.
Dinosaurs dancing in the morning dew.

Di–dino–dinosaurs dancing.
Dinosaurs dancing I see 3.
Dinosaurs dance.
Dance, dance, dancing.
Dinosaurs dancing for you and me.
La, la, la, la 1.
La, la, la, la 2.
La, la, la, la 3.
Dinosaurs dancing for you and me.

Di–dino–dinosaurs dancing.
Dinosaurs dancing I see 4.
Dinosaurs dance.
Dance, dance, dancing.
Dinosaurs dancing out the kitchen door.
La, la, la, la 1.
La, la, la, la 2.
La, la, la, la 3.
La, la, la, la 4.
Dinosaurs dancing out the kitchen door.

Di–dino–dinosaurs dancing.
Dinosaurs dancing I see 5.
Dinosaurs dance.
Dance, dance, dancing.
Dinosaurs dancing to the music live.
La, la, la, la 1.
La, la, la, la 2.
La, la, la, la 3.
La, la, la, la 4.
La, la, la, la 5.
Dinosaurs dancing to the music live.

Di–dino–dinosaurs dancing.
Dinosaurs dancing I see 6.
Dinosaurs dance.
Dance, dance, dancing.
Dinosaurs dancing and doing tricks.
La, la, la, la 1.
La, la, la, la 2.
La, la, la, la 3.
La, la, la, la 4.
La, la, la, la 5.
La, la, la, la 6.
Dinosaurs dancing and doing tricks.

Di–dino–dinosaurs dancing.
Dinosaurs dancing I see 7.
Dinosaurs dance.
Dance, dance, dancing.
Dinosaurs dancing up to heaven.
La, la, la, la 1.
La, la, la, la 2.
La, la, la, la 3.
La, la, la, la 4.
La, la, la, la 5.
La, la, la, la 6.
La, la, la, la 7.
Dinosaurs dancing up to heaven.

Di–dino–dinosaurs dancing.
Dinosaurs dancing,
Don't make a peep.
Dinosaurs dance.
Dance, dance, dancing.
Dinosaurs dancing while I sleep.
La, la, la, la, la.
Dinosaurs dancing while I sleep.

Objectives

♪ To improve role-playing skills and enhance creativity

♪ To dramatize created characters

♪ To march to a steady beat

♪ To work as a cooperative group and follow a leader

Skills

♪ Listening

♪ Following Directions

♪ Marching

♪ Leadership

♪ Group Cooperation

Music

CD #1, Track 7: "Halloween on Parade"

Halloween on Parade

ACTIVITY

1 In advance, create a path around the classroom or outside for the class to follow as they march.

2 Ask children what kinds of characters they like to pretend to be. Have volunteers demonstrate how these characters would act or move.

3 Tell the class the song they are going to hear is about dressing up and pretending. Ask them to listen for the pretend characters in the song and act out movements to represent each character as they march in their "Halloween Parade."

4 Have children stand in place and practice marching as a group. Use voice commands (e.g., *Left, right!* or *Step, step!*) as appropriate to help children find the beat to march together.

5 Line up the class. Have children place their right hand on the shoulder of the person in front of them. Instruct them to drop their hands to their sides.

6 Play the song "Halloween on Parade" as the class marches to the music and acts out the characters. Have children practice until they are comfortable with the music.

EXTENSIONS

• Have a volunteer lead the march. Repeat the activity until all children have had an opportunity to be the leader.

• Create hats and headgear, streamers and flags, or costumes for the class to wear as they march to the music. This song makes a great backdrop for school-wide Halloween parades or fall festivals.

Halloween on Parade

Words and Music by Greg Scelsa
Copyright 1989, Little House Music (ASCAP)

You can be something silly,
Like a funny ol' circus clown.
Or you can be something from
   a storybook,
Like a king or a queen with a crown.

You can be a superhero
Like the kind in a comic book.
Or you can be something a little
   bit scary,
But a little friendly, too.

You can get dressed up,
In costumes and make-up.
You know that it's only pretend
And march all around to the
   happy sounds.
The fun will never end.

Chorus:
   Halloween's on parade,
   Halloween's on parade.
   You can be anything you wanna be
   When Halloween's on parade.

Halloween's on parade,
Halloween's on parade.
You can be anything you wanna be
When Halloween's on parade.

You can be something goofy,
Like an old-time movie star,
A doctor, a nurse, or a fire chief,
A driver in a racing car.

You can be a crazy creature
From way out in outer space,
Or a character from a cartoon show
With a smile upon your face.

You can get dressed up,
In costumes and make-up.
You know that it's only pretend
And march all around to the
   happy sounds.
The fun will never end.

(Chorus)

8

Body Talk

Objectives

♪ To reinforce moving to music

♪ To promote the ability to listen to directions and execute tasks

♪ To review the names of various parts of the body

Skills

♪ Listening

♪ Movement

♪ Organization

♪ Leadership

♪ Group Cooperation

Music

CD #1, Track 8: "Body Talk"

ACTIVITY

1 Stand with children in a circle. Have them stand at least an arm's length apart from each other.

2 Tell the class to listen carefully to the movements described in the song you will play.

3 Play the song "Body Talk," and have children move with you as you model the movements (shown below).

4 After the class has practiced with the music several times, stop the CD, and have each child in turn take one step into the middle of the circle, lead the rest of the class in moving a body part mentioned in the song, and then step back in line.

EXTENSION

Have children make up new body-part movements. Have them take turns creating and modeling the new movements.

LIST OF MOVEMENTS

- eyebrows
- nose
- cheeks
- mouth
- tongue
- chin
- head
- shoulders
- elbows
- hands
- fingers

- arms
- chest
- tummy
- hips
- one leg
- the other leg
- knees
- one foot
- the other foot
- whole body

Body Talk

Words and Music by Julie Weissman
Copyright 1987, Gallery of Songs (BMI)

Move your eyebrows up and down.
Everybody move your nose, like a bunny.
Move your cheeks, like a frog.

Now move your mouth, like a fish.
Move your tongue, like a lizard.
Move your chin from side to side.

Now move your head around and around slowly.
Now move your shoulders up and down, up and down.
Now move your elbows. Wiggle those elbows.

Move your hands. Shake those hands.
Everybody move your fingers. Make them wiggle.
Swing your arms. Swing them around and around.

Move your chest—in and out. Keep going. Good!
Now move your tummy. Stick it way out.
Hold it in. Good work!
Now shake those hips.
Warm up those hips from side to side.
Move them around and around.

Move one leg. Swing it gently back and forth.
Now the other leg. Try to balance.
Swing it slowly. Good work!
Move your knees. Wiggle those knees.

Now move one foot. Shake it all around.
Get ready to shake your other foot.
Move it all around. Shake it.

All right. Get ready now.
Shake your whole body out. Wiggle every part of you.
Keep going! And stop!

Give yourselves a hand, everybody. You did a great job!

9

Shaping up with Shapes

Objectives

♪ To recognize shapes (circle, square, oval, star, triangle, rectangle)

♪ To listen and follow directions in music

♪ To practice teamwork

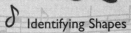

Skills

♪ Identifying Shapes

♪ Listening

♪ Teamwork

♪ Movement

Music

CD #1, Tracks 9 and 10: "Shaping up with Shapes #1" and "Shaping up with Shapes #2"

ACTIVITY

1 In advance, display one example of each shape mentioned in the objectives in different places around the room. The shapes should be within the children's reach. Also, prepare a poster or bulletin board display of all six shapes for referral.

2 Show the class examples of circles from the display. Have them find more examples of circles in the classroom. Ask them to name other places where they might see circles. Follow the same procedure with the remaining shapes.

3 Stand close to the display. Play the song "Shaping up with Shapes #1." Point to each shape as it is mentioned, and then lead the class in performing the movements described in the song.

4 Have six volunteers lead each of the six shape movements with "Shaping up with Shapes #1." Repeat with different leaders.

EXTENSIONS

• Select children to choose shapes in a random order during "Shaping up with Shapes #2" (an instrumental version of the song). Have the class say the name of each shape and then do the corresponding movement learned from "Shaping up with Shapes #1." Remind children to freeze when the music stops each time.

• Have the class play the game "Shape Races." Say a child's name, and name a shape. Time (with a stopwatch, if available) how many seconds it takes the child to reach an object of the shape named. Repeat the activity with different volunteers and shapes. Then, challenge children to reach and correctly name all six shapes.

Shaping up with Shapes

Words and Music by Steven Traugh
Copyright 1991, Kiducation (ASCAP)

Spoken:

Here's a fun game called "Shaping up with Shapes." Everyone should be standing where they have some room to safely move about. We'll call out a shape and then I'll describe a movement to do for that shape. Continue doing the movement until you hear me say "freeze." Then, you should freeze in place until we call the next shape and movement. Listen carefully and have fun!

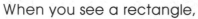

When you see a square,
Tap the top of your hair.
Tap, tap, tap, tap, tap your hair when you see a square.
Tap, tap, tap, tap, tap your hair when you see a square—freeze.

If a triangle you should see,
Then tap on both your knees.
Tap, tap, tap your knees if a triangle you should see.
Tap, tap, tap your knees if a triangle you should see—freeze.

When you see a rectangle,
Then wiggle with a jingle, jangle.
Wiggle, wiggle with a jingle, jangle when you see a rectangle.
Wiggle, wiggle with a jingle, jangle when you see a rectangle—freeze.

If an oval should appear,
Then gently pull your ears.
Pull, pull, pull, pull, pull your ears if an oval appears.
Pull, pull, pull, pull, pull your ears if an oval appears—freeze.

When you see a star,
Then lift weights with a bar.
Lift, lift, lift, lift, lift with a bar when you see a star.
Lift, lift, lift, lift, lift with a bar when you see a star—freeze.

If a circle you should spy,
Wave your arms and say, "Good-bye."
Wave, wave, wave, wave, say, "Good-bye" if a circle you spy.
Wave, wave, wave, wave, say, "Good-bye" if a circle you spy—freeze.
One more time, let's say, "Goodbye!"

Across the Bridge

Objectives

♪ To move as a group in a straight line

♪ To move sideways, leading with either the right or the left foot

Skills

♪ Coordination

♪ Movement

♪ Balance

♪ Listening

♪ Creativity

Music

CD #1, Tracks 11 and 12: "Across the Bridge #1" and "Across the Bridge #2"

ACTIVITY

1 In advance, create a "bridge" as follows:
- Place chairs in two rows to create the sides of the bridge. Use six to ten chairs in each row.
- Face each row of chairs outward so that the backs of the chairs in one row face the backs of the chairs in the other row.
- Have children walk between the two rows of chairs when they cross the bridge.

2 Have children stand and form a single line beginning at the entrance to the bridge. Play the song "Across the Bridge #1," and have children practice crossing the bridge in the following ways:
- walk across
- walk sideways, left foot first
- walk sideways, right foot first
- take giant steps

3 Stand at the entrance to the bridge, and model how to cross the bridge in the desired manner.

4 Each child should cross the bridge and then go to the end of the line to prepare for his or her next turn.

EXTENSION

Help children create other ways to cross the bridge. For example, they could
- tiptoe
- skip
- hop
- walk backward
- dance
- flap their arms and pretend to fly
- pretend to skate
- walk on all fours
- pretend to swim
- jog

Make a list of the movements they create. Play "Across the Bridge #2" (an instrumental version of the song), and direct children to cross the bridge and perform each new movement.

Across the Bridge

Words and Music by Greg Scelsa
Copyright 1980, Little House Music and Gregorian Chance Music (ASCAP)

Across the bridge, across the bridge,
C'mon and take a turn and go across the bridge.
Across the bridge, across the bridge,
But don't fall in the water goin' across the bridge.

Spoken:
All right everybody, walk across the bridge.

Across the bridge, across the bridge,
C'mon and take a turn and go across the bridge.
Across the bridge, across the bridge,
But don't fall in the water goin' across the bridge.

Spoken:
Walk sideways across the bridge, left foot first.

Across the bridge, across the bridge,
C'mon and take a turn and go across the bridge.
Across the bridge, across the bridge,
But don't fall in the water goin' across the bridge.

Spoken:
Now walk sideways across the bridge, right foot first.

Across the bridge, across the bridge,
C'mon and take a turn and go across the bridge.
Across the bridge, across the bridge,
But don't fall in the water goin' across the bridge.

Spoken:
Take giant steps across the bridge.

Across the bridge, across the bridge,
C'mon and take a turn and go across the bridge.
Across the bridge, across the bridge,
But don't fall in the water goin' across the bridge.

11

Counting up to Twenty

Objectives

♪ To improve counting skills

♪ To improve singing skills

Skills

♪ Counting

♪ Singing

Music

CD #1, Track 13: "Counting up to Twenty"

ACTIVITY

1 In advance, display the numbers 1 through 20 on a chalkboard or chart paper as shown on the lyric page.

2 Play the song "Counting up to Twenty." Lead the class in echo and unison singing as you track the numbers and words on your display in time with the music. Repeat as desired.

3 Have a volunteer point to the numbers on the display and lead the class in singing with the music. Have new volunteers repeat the activity.

EXTENSIONS

• Replace the numerals on your display with number words (e.g., one, two, three), and have the class practice reading the number words as they sing with the music.

• Make number cards for 1–20. Write each numeral on one side and the corresponding number word on the other side. Select 20 children to display the cards at the front of the classroom. Play "Counting up to Twenty," and lead the volunteers in raising their cards high in time with the lyrics. Have them alternate between displaying the numeral and the number word. Repeat as desired.

• Make up movements to lead during the chorus section of the song.

• Hand out number cards for 1, 5, 10, 15, and 20 to volunteers. Have the volunteers stand in a line facing the class. Be sure to leave enough space between each child to fit classmates with the remaining numbers. Hand out the remaining cards in random order. Help each child find his or her numerical position in line to create the sequence 1 through 20.

Counting up to Twenty

Words and Music by Steven Traugh
Copyright 1991, Kiducation (ASCAP)

1, 2, 3

4, 5, 6

7, 8, 9

10, 11, 12

13, 14

15, 16

17, 18

19, 20

Counting up to 20,
Come sing along with me.
Counting up to 20,
We'll do it easily.

Alphabet Soup

Objectives

♪ To learn the alphabet through singing

♪ To improve singing skills

Skills

♪ Singing

♪ Reading

♪ Counting

Music

CD #1, Track 14: "Alphabet Soup"

ACTIVITY

1 In advance, create an alphabet chart as shown below. You may choose to use lowercase letters instead. Post the chart where the class can easily read it.

A B C D
E F G H
I J K L
M N O P
Q R S T
U V W
X Y Z

2 Play the song "Alphabet Soup." During the chorus, lead the class in the movements described in the song.

3 Point to the letters on your alphabet chart as you lead children in singing each verse. Repeat as desired.

EXTENSION

Make individual lowercase letter squares about 4" (10 cm) in size. Have a bulletin board or pocket chart prepared with uppercase letters in sequential order. Hand out the lowercase letter squares. Have children identify their letters, one at a time, and match them to the corresponding uppercase letter.

Alphabet Soup

Words and Music by Steven Traugh
Copyright 1990, Kiducation (ASCAP)

Alphabet soup, alphabet soup,
Oh, how we love our alphabet soup.

Look at all the letters floating in this goop.
Let's try and read our alphabet soup.

(sway arms from side to side)
(clasp hands together and press against heart)

(cup hands above eyes and look down)
(draw horizontal circle—the soup bowl—at your waist)

A – B – C – D
E – F – G – H
I – J – K – L
M – N – O – P
Q – R – S – T
U – V – W
X – Y – Z

All together now!

A – B – C – D – E – F – G – H
I – J – K – L – M – N – O – P
Q – R – S – T – U – V – W
X – Y – Z

One more time!

A – B – C – D – E – F – G – H
I – J – K – L – M – N – O – P
Q – R – S – T – U – V – W
X – Y – Z

Alphabet soup, alphabet soup,
Oh, how we love our alphabet soup.
Look at all the letters floating in this goop.
Let's try and read our
Alphabet, alphabet, alphabet, alphabet, alphabet soup.

13

Bingo

Objectives

♪ To clap a rhythm pattern that grows in length

♪ To sing the song "Bingo"

Skills

♪ Rhythm

♪ Spelling

♪ Singing

Music

CD #1, Track 15: "Bingo"

ACTIVITY

1 Write *BINGO* in large, well-spaced letters on a chalkboard or chart paper.

2 Tell the class that they are about to learn a song about a dog named Bingo.

3 Have children read aloud each letter.

4 Play the song "Bingo." Point to each letter in the word *BINGO* as it is sung. Each new verse features a different musical accent (i.e., clapping once for each letter that is omitted).

5 Play the song again, and have children clap on the missing letters as they are left out of the song. Point to the letter being left out as the class sings. Draw a slash (/) across each successive letter to be replaced with a musical accent. Point out to children that the rhythm in which the letters are sung is not a steady beat. The letters "B" and "I" occur at the same speed, but the letters "N–G–O" occur twice as fast, creating a rhythm pattern that children must learn to clap. Teach children to sing "Bingo" slowly without the music. Have them concentrate on clapping (and not singing) the letters to be left out. Play the song again.

EXTENSIONS

• Have volunteers lead the class in singing and clapping the song.

• Write *BINGO* on a chalkboard or chart paper. Play the song, and have a child cross out each letter at the appropriate time. Lead the class in singing and clapping in time with the music. You may wish to pick two leaders at a time. Have one leader cross out the letter while the other leads the class in clapping and singing. Choose new leaders, and repeat as desired.

• Help the class make up other five-letter names for the dog. Make a list of their suggestions. Write one of the names on a chalkboard or chart paper. Lead the class in singing "Bingo" with the new name. Cross out each letter of the new name at the appropriate time in the song. Have the class clap out the name.

Bingo

Adapted and arranged by Greg Scelsa
Copyright 1980, Little House Music and
Gregorian Chance Music (ASCAP)

There was a farmer had a dog,
And Bingo was his name, oh!
B, I, N, G, O!
B, I, N, G, O!
B, I, N, G, O!
And Bingo was his name, oh!

There was a farmer had a dog,
And Bingo was his name, oh!
(Clap) I, N, G, O!
(Clap) I, N, G, O!
(Clap) I, N, G, O!
And Bingo was his name, oh!

There was a farmer had a dog,
And Bingo was his name, oh!
(Clap, clap) N, G, O!
(Clap, clap) N, G, O!
(Clap, clap) N, G, O!
And Bingo was his name, oh!

There was a farmer had a dog,
And Bingo was his name, oh!
(Clap, clap, clap) G, O!
(Clap, clap, clap) G, O!
(Clap, clap, clap) G, O!
And Bingo was his name, oh!

There was a farmer had a dog,
And Bingo was his name, oh!
(Clap, clap, clap, clap) O!
(Clap, clap, clap, clap) O!
(Clap, clap, clap, clap) O!
And Bingo was his name, oh!

There was a farmer had a dog,
And Bingo was his name, oh!
(Clap, clap, clap, clap, clap)
(Clap, clap, clap, clap, clap)
(Clap, clap, clap, clap, clap)
And Bingo was his name, oh!

14

The Name Clapping Game

Objectives

♪ To have children spell their own names and the names of other classmates

♪ To improve rhythmic skills

♪ To improve singing skills

Skills

♪ Spelling

♪ Reading

♪ Rhythm

♪ Singing

Music

CD #1, Track 16: "The Name Clapping Game"

ACTIVITY

1 In advance, write the ten names mentioned in the song "The Name Clapping Game" on a chalkboard or chart paper. Add the names of five children in your class to the list. Practice singing the children's names to the music before introducing this lesson to the class.

2 Play "The Name Clapping Game," and point to the letters of each name in time with the lyrics. Have children clap in rhythm as you point to each letter.

3 During the second half of the song, lead the class in singing and clapping the names of their classmates.

4 Repeat the activity with the names of new children until everyone has been named.

EXTENSIONS

• After the class has mastered the names of all their classmates, have them substitute the names of family members or pets in the second half of the song.

• Create a new subject for the clapping game (e.g., The Color Clapping Game, The Number Clapping Game, The Food Clapping Game). Display a list of related words for children to plug into the melody. Lead the class in singing the new song without the music.

The Name Clapping Game

Words by Steven Traugh
Copyright 1990, Kiducation (ASCAP)

I'll sing and clap with my new friend,
And Amy is her name, oh!
A – M – Y
A – M – Y
A – M – Y
And Amy is her name, oh!

I'll sing and clap with my new friend,
And Paul is his name, oh!
P – A – U – L
P – A – U – L
P – A – U – L
And Paul is his name, oh!

I'll sing and clap with my new friend,
And Maria is her name, oh!
M – A – R – I – A
M – A – R – I – A
M – A – R – I – A
And Maria is her name, oh!

I'll sing and clap with my new friend,
And Bobby is his name, oh!
B – O – B – B – Y
B – O – B – B – Y
B – O – B – B – Y
And Bobby is his name, oh!

I'll sing and clap with my new friend,
And Ashley is her name, oh!
A – S – H – L – E – Y
A – S – H – L – E – Y
A – S – H – L – E – Y
And Ashley is her name, oh!

I'll sing and clap with my new friend,
And Marcus is his name, oh!
M – A – R – C – U – S
M – A – R – C – U – S
M – A – R – C – U – S
And Marcus is his name, oh!

I'll sing and clap with my new friend,
And Melinda is her name, oh!
M – E – L – I – N – D – A
M – E – L – I – N – D – A
M – E – L – I – N – D – A
And Melinda is her name, oh!

I'll sing and clap with my new friend,
And Hiroshi is his name, oh!
H – I – R – O – S – H – I
H – I – R – O – S – H – I
H – I – R – O – S – H – I
And Hiroshi is his name, oh!

I'll sing and clap with my new friend,
And Courtney is her name, oh!
C – O – U – R – T – N – E – Y
C – O – U – R – T – N – E – Y
C – O – U – R – T – N – E – Y
And Courtney is her name, oh!

I'll sing and clap with my new friend,
And Jonathan is his name, oh!
J – O – N – A – T – H – A – N
J – O – N – A – T – H – A – N
J – O – N – A – T – H – A – N
And Jonathan is his name, oh!

New Zoo Review

Objectives

♪ To create movements to dramatize the beat and mood of the music

♪ To move like various zoo animals

♪ To extend movement vocabulary

Skills

♪ Movement

♪ Vocabulary

♪ Teamwork

Music

CD #1, Track 17: "New Zoo Review"

ACTIVITY

1 In advance, create a list of the animals named in the song "New Zoo Review." Add pictures if you wish.

2 Play "New Zoo Review," and display the list. Point to each animal on the list and lead the class in moving as that animal to the music. Repeat as desired.

3 Have volunteers lead the class in the movements to the music. Invite new leaders to repeat the activity.

EXTENSIONS

• Have children use words to describe the movements of each animal (e.g., an elephant's movements might be slow, heavy, and long; a monkey's fast, light, and quick).

• Have children work in pairs to create movements that are opposite from each other (e.g., fast/slow, continuous/broken, loud/quiet). Invite each pair to demonstrate for the group, and have the class try to identify the two movements.

• Ask the class to name some of their favorite zoo animals. Have volunteers move as their favorite animal might move.

• Have children paint pictures of their favorite zoo animals. Encourage them to use swirls, splashes, dots, and squiggles to show the movement of the animals.

New Zoo Review

Words and Music by Greg Scelsa
Copyright 1997, Kazoo Music (ASCAP)

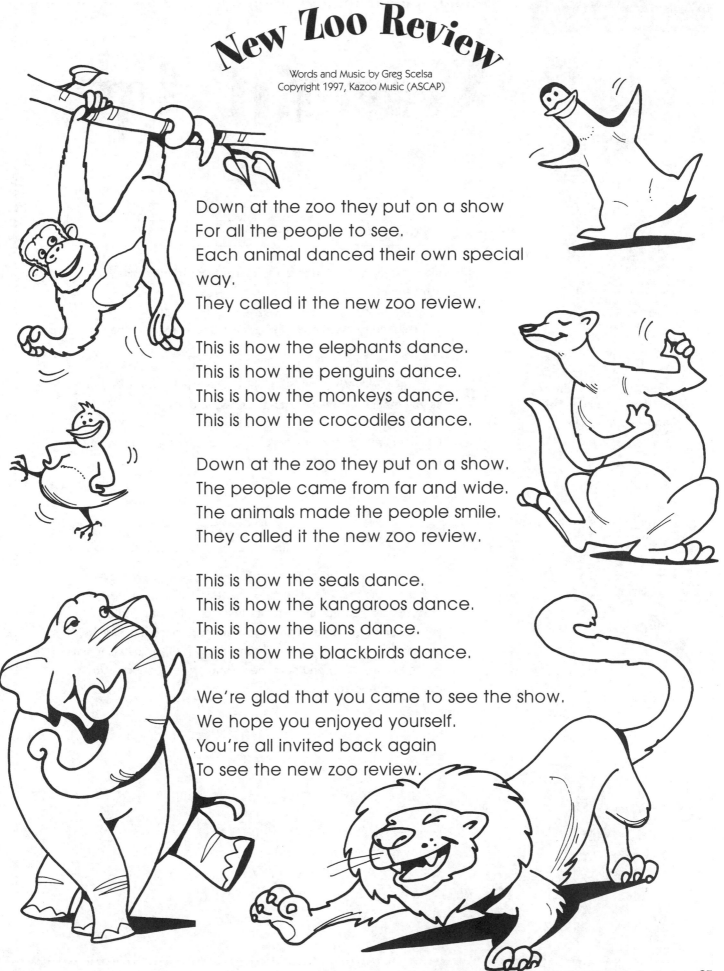

Down at the zoo they put on a show
For all the people to see.
Each animal danced their own special way.
They called it the new zoo review.

This is how the elephants dance.
This is how the penguins dance.
This is how the monkeys dance.
This is how the crocodiles dance.

Down at the zoo they put on a show.
The people came from far and wide.
The animals made the people smile.
They called it the new zoo review.

This is how the seals dance.
This is how the kangaroos dance.
This is how the lions dance.
This is how the blackbirds dance.

We're glad that you came to see the show.
We hope you enjoyed yourself.
You're all invited back again
To see the new zoo review.

16

Warmin' Up

Objectives

♪ To improve moving to music

♪ To promote the ability to listen to directions and execute tasks

Skills

♪ Listening

♪ Movement

♪ Expression

♪ Rhythm

Music

CD #2, Tracks 1 and 2: "Warmin' Up #1" and "Warmin' Up #2"

ACTIVITY

1 Have the class stand in an area where they can move their arms freely.

2 Tell children to listen carefully to the movements described in the song you will play.

3 Play the song "Warmin' Up #1." Have the class move with you as you model the movements described in the song.

4 Choose eight volunteers to model each of the eight movements in the song, and repeat the activity.

EXTENSION

Have volunteers take turns creating and modeling new movements for the rest of the class to imitate. Challenge children to create "theme based" movements. For example, they could create animal movements, sport movements, dance movements, and machine movements. Play "Warmin' Up #2" (an instrumental version of the song), and have the volunteers lead the class in the new movements.

Warmin' Up

Words and Music by Greg Scelsa
Copyright 1983, '84 & '86, Gregorian Chance Music and Little
House Music (ASCAP)

Spoken:
*All right, everybody, it's time to get up and get loose. So stand up straight
and tall and just follow my directions 'cause we're warmin' up!*

Pretend there's a long rope hanging down just for you.
Reach up and grab it. Now pull yourself up on that rope.
Reach, reach. Higher. Come on, stretch, stretch.
Reach up there now. Stand on your toes and reach, reach.
Good, keep going now, higher. Yeah.

Now, put your hands at your sides and roll your head around . . .
All the way around. Don't get dizzy now.
Good, keep going, around and around. Yeah.

Now, push both shoulders up as high as you can.
Make 'em touch your ears, good. Now, let 'em down.
Now, push your shoulders up again. Make 'em touch your ears.
Good, now, let 'em down again. Now, let's do it again.
Go up, down, up, down, up, down, up, down. Keep going. Good.

Now, pretend like you're swimming in the water.
Make your arms move just like you're swimming.
Swim, swim, swim. Good work, now, swim.

Now, shake your hands out really fast. Come on, shake 'em.
Faster! Shake 'em faster. Good.
Now, make both arms flop around just like they have no bones,
Like floppy wet spaghetti. Flop 'em around.
Now, shake both hands out again. Faster, yeah!
Now, make them like floppy wet spaghetti again.
Flop 'em around.

Now, everybody stand up straight and tall.
Put your hands on your waist and bend at the waist,
All the way around,
To the front, side, back,
All the way around and around.

Now, shake one leg out real fast. Shake a leg. Faster. Good.
Now, slow it down and make it wiggle really slow. Make it wiggle.
Now, shake the other leg out. Shake it out.
Come on now, let's see you shake.
O.K. Now, slow it down again. Make it wiggle really slow. Good.

Now, everybody shake your whole body out.
Come on, everybody shake it out.
Now, stand still.
Everybody freeze like a statue.

17

Days of the Week

Objective

♪ To sing the days of the week

Skills

♪ Singing

♪ Movement

♪ Reading

Music

CD #2, Tracks 3 and 4: "Days of the Week #1" and "Days of the Week #2"

ACTIVITY

1 Recite each line of the song "Days of the Week #1," and have the class echo in response after each line. Put up one finger for each day you recite. Have children do the same in response.

2 Have children practice singing the song with the music.

3 Allow children to make up movements to dramatize the second verse of the song.

EXTENSIONS

• Teach the class the days of the week in Spanish: lunes, martes, miércoles, jueves, viernes, sábado, domingo. Play the Spanish version of the song, "Days of the Week #2," and have the class sing along.

• Give each child a copy of the Munchie Monster reproducible (page 63). Read aloud the words, and discuss the pictures. Have children color and cut out the food pieces and then glue each one above the corresponding day of the week.

Days of the Week

Words and Music by Christopher and Covita Moroney
Copyright 1980, Little House Music (ASCAP)

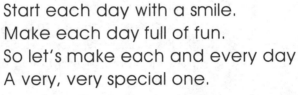

Days of the Week #1

Monday, Tuesday,
Wednesday, Thursday, Friday,
Saturday, and Sunday.
The days of the week.

(Repeat)

Start each day with a smile.
Make each day full of fun.
So let's make each and every day
A very, very special one.

(Repeat)

The days of the week!

Days of the Week #2

Lunes, martes,
miércoles, jueves, viernes,
sábado, y domingo.
The days of the week.

(Repeat)

Start each day with a smile.
Make each day full of fun.
So let's make each and every day
A very, very special one.

(Repeat)

The days of the week!

18

Rock 'Round the Mulberry Bush

Objectives

♪ To reinforce through dramatization good health and personal hygiene habits

♪ To synchronize movements to the music of "Rock 'Round the Mulberry Bush"

Skills

♪ Keeping Steady Beat

♪ Rhythmic Coordination

♪ Creativity

Music

CD #2, Tracks 5 and 6: "Rock 'Round the Mulberry Bush #1" and "Rock 'Round the Mulberry Bush #2"

ACTIVITY

1 Have the class join hands with you and form a circle. Teach them the following movements:
- Have children take one step sideways to the left and stop with their feet apart while saying *step*.
- Have them bring their right foot over to their left foot and say *together*.
- Have children repeat this two-beat movement combination to the left while repeating *step, together, step, together*.
- Have children go very slowly at first. Make sure everyone is saying *step, together* out loud. Remember that most children are more coordinated with their mouth than with their feet. The children having difficulty are usually not saying the words aloud.

2 Read the first line of each of the seven verses in the song "Rock 'Round the Mulberry Bush" one at a time. Ask children to suggest movements that depict each activity. Teach the class the movements suggested.

3 Play "Rock 'Round the Mulberry Bush #1." Lead the class in performing the movements they created. Repeat as desired.

EXTENSIONS

- Have volunteers take turns leading the movements to the song. Encourage children to sing along with the music as they perform the movements.

- Discuss other hygiene activities with the class, and have children make up movements to dramatize each activity (e.g., washing dishes, cleaning house, or shampooing their hair). Invite the class to perform these new movements with "Rock 'Round the Mulberry Bush #2," an instrumental version of the song.

Rock 'Round the Mulberry Bush

Adapted by Greg Scelsa
Copyright 1979, Little House Music and
Gregorian Chance Music (ASCAP)

Chorus:
Rock 'round the mulberry bush.
Let's rock 'round the mulberry bush.
Let's rock 'round the mulberry bush,
So early in the morning.

(Hold hands in a circle and sidestep to the left in time with music. Repeat "Step, together, step, together" to the end of the chorus.)

This is the way we all wake up,
All wake up, all wake up.
This is the way we all wake up,
So early in the morning.

(Yawn and stretch. Reach high with both hands. Rub the sleep out of your eyes.)

(Join hands during this line.)

(Chorus)

(Sidestep left in the circle.)

This is the way we make our bed,
Make our bed, make our bed.
This is the way we make our bed,
So early in the morning.

(Pull up, straighten and smooth the covers, fluff the pillows, and place them at the head of the bed.)
(Join hands during this line.)

(Chorus)

(Sidestep left in the circle.)

This is the way we wash our face,
Wash our face, wash our face.
This is the way we wash our face,
So early in the morning.

(Turn on water, wet and soap washcloth, wash face, rinse cloth, rinse face, and turn off water.)
(Join hands during this line.)

(Chorus)

(Sidestep left in the circle.)

This is the way we brush our teeth,
Brush our teeth, brush our teeth.
This is the way we brush our teeth,
So early in the morning.

(Hold toothbrush, apply toothpaste, brush teeth up and down, in and out, then spit.)

(Join hands during this line.)

(Chorus)

(Sidestep left in the circle.)

This is the way we take a bath,
Take a bath, take a bath.
This is the way we take a bath,
So early in the morning.

(Dip into the tub, soap washcloth, and wash arms, torso, legs, and bottom.)

(Join hands during this line.)

(Chorus)

(Sidestep left in the circle.)

This is the way we comb our hair,
Comb our hair, comb our hair.
This is the way we comb our hair,
So early in the morning.

(Pick up comb. Look into mirror. Comb hair up, back, and on the sides. Smile approvingly.)
(Join hands during this line.)

(Chorus)

(Sidestep left in the circle.)

This is the way we wash our hands,
Wash our hands, wash our hands.
This is the way we wash our hands,
So early in the morning.

(Turn on water, pick up soap, lather hands put down soap, shake.)

(Join hands during this line.)

(Chorus)

(Sidestep left in the circle.)

Objectives

♪ To dramatize the lyrics of a song

♪ To improve singing skills

♪ To memorize and follow a series of movements

♪ To improve language arts skills

Skills

♪ Listening

♪ Movement

♪ Singing

♪ Reading

♪ Writing Creatively

Music

CD #2, Track 7: "What Will We Do When We All Go Out to Play?"

What Will We Do When We All Go Out to Play?

ACTIVITY

1 In advance, write the lyrics to the song "What Will We Do When We All Go Out to Play?" on a chalkboard or chart paper.

2 Read aloud the lyrics one line at a time. Have children echo each line after you. Have volunteers act out each activity (e.g., bounce a ball, ride a bike). Have children use the created movements for each line to help them memorize the lyrics.

3 Next, play "What Will We Do When We All Go Out to Play?" Have the class sing and use their created movements to act out the song. Repeat as desired.

EXTENSIONS

• Have each small group of children illustrate an activity in the song. Use their pictures to create a montage. Write the appropriate lyric at the bottom of each page, and bind the pages into a class book titled *What Will We Do When We All Go Out to Play?*

• Create a "When We All Go Out to Play" obstacle course for children on the playground. Create separate stations where children bounce a ball, ride a real or an imaginary bike, swing on a swing ten times, and then run to a bench and pretend to row a boat ten times.

• Discuss the importance of safety and why rules help us. Help children create a list of safety rules. Have each small group of children illustrate a rule. Use the illustrations to create a bulletin board on safety.

What Will We Do When We All Go Out to Play?

Words and Music by Greg Scelsa
Copyright 1997, Kazoo Music/Little House Music (ASCAP)

What will we do when we all go out,
All go out, all go out?
What will we do when we all go out,
When we all go out to play?

I'm gonna bounce a rubber ball,
A rubber ball, a rubber ball.
I'm gonna bounce a rubber ball
When we all go out to play.

I'm gonna ride on a bike,
On a bike, on a bike.
I'm gonna ride on a bike
When we all go out to play.

I'm gonna swing on a swing,
On a swing, on a swing.
I'm gonna swing on a swing
When we all go out to play.

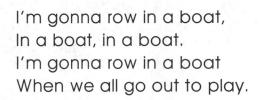

I'm gonna row in a boat,
In a boat, in a boat.
I'm gonna row in a boat
When we all go out to play.

I'm gonna dig in the sand,
In the sand, in the sand.
I'm gonna dig in the sand
When we all go out to play.

I'm gonna climb on a ladder,
On a ladder, on a ladder.
I'm gonna climb on a ladder
When we all go out to play.

20

Listen and Move

Objective

♪ To learn a variety of ambulatory movements

Skills

♪ Aural Retention

♪ Rhythmic Coordination

♪ Movement

♪ Concentration

Music

CD #2, Track 8: "Listen and Move"

ACTIVITY

1 Tell the class they are going to learn to move with several different pieces of music.

2 Help children create movements for each of the six pieces of music in the song "Listen and Move." The spoken cues will direct children to walk, gallop, tiptoe, run, skate, and hop.

3 Play "Listen and Move." Lead the class in performing the movements they created, and have children do the movements in place.

4 Encourage children to do each movement in time with the music.

5 Play only the first half of "Listen and Move." Pause the music after children are finished hopping.

6 Tell the class that they will now hear the same music, but without any direction as to which movement to do. They must listen and try to remember which movement goes with each piece of music.

7 Play the second half of the song. Have children practice improving the quality and timing of the movements.

EXTENSION

Select six volunteers who each wish to lead a movement to one of the pieces of music in "Listen and Move." Have the leaders stand and face the class in the order of the music selections. Play the song, and have each leader step forward and lead the class in turn. Have new leaders repeat the activity.

Listen and Move

Music by Greg Scelsa
Copyright 1978, Little House Music and
Gregorian Chance Music (ASCAP)

Instrumental with spoken cues

1st rhythm—walk

2nd rhythm—gallop

3rd rhythm—tiptoe

4th rhythm—run

5th rhythm—skate

6th rhythm—hop

Quiet Time

ACTIVITY

1 Have the class stand where they have room to move their arms and legs.

2 Tell children that they are about to practice moving in slow motion.

3 Play the instrumental song "Quiet Time," and lead children in slow motion movements. Use the following sequence as a guide:
- move fingers (on one hand and then both hands)
- move arms (one and then both)
- move head (include facial expressions)
- move upper torso
- move legs and feet (one and then both)
- move combinations of body parts

4 Demonstrate movements that show familiar actions in slow motion. Ask the class to watch carefully and try to identify each activity. Activities may include the following:
- vacuum a rug
- unlock and open a door
- make a sandwich and take a bite
- cast a line and catch a fish
- look up a telephone number and make a call

5 Help children create a list of activities they might act out with slow motion movements. Write the list on a chalkboard or chart paper.

6 Have volunteers model one of the activities on the list. Instruct the rest of the class to imitate the movements.

7 Have children practice these movements with and without the music.

Quiet Time
Music by Greg Scelsa
Copyright 1975, Little House Music and Gregorian Chance Music (ASCAP)

Objectives

♪ To move in slow motion

♪ To create movements that tell a story or describe an action

Skills

♪ Concentration

♪ Movement

♪ Coordination

♪ Creativity

Music

CD #2, Track 9:
"Quiet Time"

A-Hunting We Will Go

ACTIVITY

1 Tell the class that they are now going to learn to move and sing to the song "A-Hunting We Will Go."

2 Read each line of the first verse. Have the class echo in response.

3 Read the words to the entire song, one verse at a time, and help children create movements for the actions described.

4 Lead the class in performing the movements with the song "A-Hunting We Will Go #1."

5 Have children practice doing the movements they created while singing along with the music. Repeat as desired.

6 Have eight volunteers stand in a line facing the rest of the class. Play "A-Hunting We Will Go #1." Have each leader in turn step forward and lead the chosen movement. Invite new leaders to repeat the activity.

EXTENSIONS

• Write the lyrics on sentence strips. Display the sentence strips in a pocket chart, and track the words as the children sing along with the music.

• Change the title and subject of the song to A-Reading, A-Flying, or A-Dancing We Will Go, and have children write verses for the new topic. Invite them to illustrate their new verses, and use their work for a Big Book or bulletin board activity. Have the class sing and dramatize the new verses with "A-Hunting We Will Go #2" (an instrumental version of the song).

Objectives

♪ To create movements to dramatize the lyrics of a song

♪ To improve singing skills

♪ To rewrite the lyrics of a song

Skills

♪ Dramatic Expression

♪ Singing

♪ Creative Writing

Music

CD #2, Tracks 10 and 11: "A-Hunting We Will Go #1" and "A-Hunting We Will Go #2"

A-Hunting We Will Go

Words and Music by Steven Traugh
Copyright 1988, Kiducation

Oh, a-hunting we will go,
A-hunting we will go.
We'll catch a fox
And put him in a box,
And then we'll let him go!

Oh, a-hunting we will go,
A-hunting we will go.
We'll catch a cat
And put him in a hat,
And then we'll let him go!

Oh, a-hunting we will go,
A-hunting we will go.
We'll catch a mouse
And put him in a house,
And then we'll let him go!

Oh, a-hunting we will go,
A-hunting we will go.
We'll catch a goat
And put him in a boat,
And then we'll let him go!

Oh, a-hunting we will go,
A-hunting we will go.
We'll catch a bear
And take him to the fair,
And then we'll let him go!

Oh, a-hunting we will go,
A-hunting we will go.
We'll catch a mongoose
And feed him apple juice,
And then we'll let him go!

Oh, a-hunting we will go,
A-hunting we will go.
We'll catch a stegosaurus
And make him dance for us,
And then we'll let him go!

Oh, a-hunting we will go,
A-hunting we will go.
We'll catch a hippopotamus
And try to put him on a bus,
And then we'll let him go!

The Beanbag Boogie

ACTIVITY

1 In advance, find a beanbag for each child, or use these ideas to create your own beanbags:
- Partially fill socks with beans or rice, and close the ends of the socks with a knot or a twist tie.
- Fill resealable plastic bags with beans or rice, and tightly seal them. Use tape to keep the seal from opening.

2 Tell the class that they will play a game in which they must balance a beanbag on various parts of their body and move at the same time. Give each child a beanbag.

3 Have children practice each movement slowly without the music in the following sequence:
- beanbag on head
- beanbag on shoulder
- beanbag on elbow
- jumping movement
- beanbag on forehead
- beanbag on index finger
- beanbag on ear
- shaking movement
- beanbag on tummy
- beanbag on back
- beanbag on knee
- stomping movement

4 Play the song "The Beanbag Boogie," and have children follow the directions given in the song. During each chorus, children must balance their beanbag and jump, shake, or stomp as directed. Repeat as desired.

EXTENSIONS

- Have children create dance movements that involve passing or tossing the beanbag from one person to the next.

- Have volunteers lead the movements. Practice with and without the music.

Objectives

♪ To create movements while balancing a beanbag on various parts of the body

♪ To improve coordination and balancing skills

Skills

♪ Balance

♪ Coordination

♪ Concentration

♪ Creativity

Music

CD #2, Track 12: "The Beanbag Boogie"

The Beanbag Boogie

Words and Music by Greg Scelsa
Copyright 1987, Treasury of Tunes (ASCAP)

Put your beanbag on your head,
While you move your body to the sound.
Now put your beanbag on your shoulder.
Don't let your beanbag touch the ground.
Now put your beanbag on your elbow,
And move your body all around.
Yeah! Yeah!
Now hold that beanbag in your hand,
And boogie while you can.

Chorus:
   Come on and jump to the beanbag boogie,
   Come on and jump to the beanbag boogie.
   Everybody jump to the beanbag boogie.
   Come on and jump to the beanbag boogie.

Put your beanbag on your forehead,
While you move any way you choose.
Now put your beanbag on your finger,
And get your whole self in the groove.
Now put your beanbag on your ear,
And let the music make you move.
Wow! Wow!
Now hold that beanbag in your hand,
And boogie while you can.

(Chorus—shake)

Put that beanbag on your tummy,
Lean back and boogie to the sound.
Put that beanbag on your back.
Remember, don't let it touch the ground.
Now put that beanbag on your knee,
And boogie, boogie to the sound.
Oh yeah!
Now hold that beanbag in your hand,
And boogie while you can.

(Chorus—stomp)

Skip to My Loo

ACTIVITY

1 Have children join hands in a circle. Have them practice skipping around the circle to the right.

2 Read aloud the following lines from "Skip to My Loo," and model the movements described:
- touch your toes and reach to the sky
- flap your wings and fly like a bird
- paint with a paintbrush
- bang your drum with a boom, boom, boom
- come to the middle and all join hands

3 When children have learned the movements, have them practice the following sequence:
- skip around the circle to the right
- touch your toes and reach to the sky
- skip around the circle to the right
- flap your wings and fly like a bird
- skip around the circle to the right
- paint with a paintbrush
- skip around the circle to the right
- bang your drum with a boom, boom, boom
- skip around the circle to the right
- come to the middle and all join hands
- skip around the circle to the right

4 Play the song "Skip to My Loo #1," and lead the class in performing the movements with the music. Repeat as desired.

EXTENSION

Help the class create six different movements to perform with the music. Illustrate and label each movement. Have children practice the new movements with "Skip to My Loo #2" (an instrumental version of the song).

Objectives

♪ To create movements described in the song "Skip to My Loo"

♪ To execute these movements in time with the beat

Skills

♪ Listening

♪ Movement

♪ Rhythm

♪ Coordination

Music

CD #2, Tracks 13 and 14: "Skip to My Loo #1" and "Skip to My Loo #2"

Skip to My Loo

Adapted by Steve Millang and Greg Scelsa
Copyright 1975, Little House Music (ASCAP)

Chorus:
    Loo-loo, skip to my loo,
    Loo-loo, skip to my loo,
    Loo-loo, skip to my loo,
    Skip to my loo, my loo-loo.

(Call to the children to come to the circle from their seats and all join hands.)

'Round in a circle, 'round and 'round,
'Round in a circle, 'round and 'round,
'Round in a circle, 'round and 'round,
Skip to my loo, my loo-loo.

(Everyone turns and skips to the right while holding hands.)

(Chorus)

(Continue skipping in a circle to the right, holding hands.)

Touch your toes and reach to the sky,
Touch your toes and reach to the sky,
Touch your toes and reach to the sky,
Skip to my loo, my loo-loo.

(Bend over and touch toes—with knees bent—then reach high on tiptoes. Repeat 3 times.)
(Join hands.)

(Chorus)

(Skip around the circle to the right.)

Flap your wings and fly like a bird,
Flap your wings and fly like a bird,
Flap your wings and fly like a bird,
Skip to my loo, my loo-loo.

(Fold your arms in and put your thumbs under your shoulder. Flap your arms up and down. Repeat three times.)
(Join hands.)

(Chorus)

(Skip around the circle to the right.)

Paint with a paintbrush, ch-ch-ch,
Paint with a paintbrush, ch-ch-ch,
Paint with a paintbrush, ch-ch-ch,
Skip to my loo, my loo-loo.

(Pretend to hold a paint can in one hand and a brush in the other. Dip once, brush 3 times. Repeat 3 times.)
(Join hands.)

(Chorus)

(Skip around the circle to the right.)

Bang your drum with a boom, boom, boom,
Bang your drum with a boom, boom, boom,
Bang your drum with a boom, boom, boom,
Skip to my loo, my loo-loo.

(Tap drum, alternating hands in 1, 2, cha–cha–cha rhythm. Repeat 3 times.)
(Join hands.)

(Chorus)

(Skip around the circle to the right.)

Come to the middle, all join hands,
Come to the middle, all join hands,
Come to the middle, all join hands,
Skip to my loo, my loo-loo.

(Girls step forward and clap hands, then step back.)
(Boys step forward and clap hands, then step back.)
(All step forward and clap hands then step back.)
(Join hands.)

(Chorus)

(Skip around the circle to the right.)

Riding in My Car

ACTIVITY

1 Have children sit on the floor, leaving enough space so that they can move their arms freely. Ask children to tell you all the steps necessary in order to take a car ride (e.g., open the door, get into the car, buckle the seatbelt, put the key into the ignition).

2 Write simple instructions or picture clues on the chalkboard to show the sequence of the steps the class has given you. Have volunteers come up in front of the class to demonstrate each of the steps listed on the board.

3 Display the lyrics to the song "Riding in My Car." Explain that the song tells about the sequence of steps for riding in a car. Ask the class to stand and act out the steps they hear in the lyrics.

4 Play the song, and have volunteers lead the class in moving and singing in motion with the music. Repeat as desired.

EXTENSIONS

- Help the class compare their list to the list in the song. Ask these questions:
  - Did the song leave out any important steps?
  - What steps did the song leave out?
  - Why do you think the song talked about these particular steps?
  - Is there anything else you would include?

- This song makes a great springboard to units on general safety, rules of the road, car or bicycle safety, or multistep directions.

- Have the class create posters with rules for crosswalk, bicycle, school bus, and car safety. Post their work in school hallways and classrooms.

Objectives

♪ To improve singing skills

♪ To listen and follow directions within a song

♪ To create movements to dramatize the lyrics of a song

♪ To compare and contrast steps to a car ride

Skills

♪ Singing

♪ Creative Drama

♪ Sequencing

♪ Comparison and Contrast

♪ Following Directions

Music

CD #2, Track 15: "Riding in My Car"

Riding in My Car

Words and Music by Woody Guthrie
Copyright 1969, Folkways Music

Chorus:
  Take you riding in my car, car,
  Take you riding in my car, car,
  Take you riding in my car, car,
  I'll take you riding in my car.

Spoken:
Well, this old jalopy may not be much to look at,
It sure is my pride and joy.
So open up the car door,
Jump on in,
Fasten those safety belts,
We're gonna go for a spin.

Click, clack, open up the door, girls.
Click, clack, open up the door, boys.
Front door, back door, clickety, clack,
Take you riding in my car.

(Chorus)

Spoken:
Well, to drive my car you gotta start the engine.
So everybody take your key and turn it.
Now let me hear you make that engine roar,
  broom.

The engine, it goes broom-broom.
The engine, it goes broom-broom.
Front seat, back seat, girls and boys,
Take you riding in my car.

(Chorus)

Spoken:
The horn on my car doesn't honk honk or
  beep beep.
It goes ah-hoo-ga!
All right, let me hear you make that sound.
Ah-hoo-ga, ah-hoo-ga, yeah!

I'm gonna let you blow the horn,
I'm gonna let you blow the horn,
Ah-hoo-ga, ah-hoo-ga!
Take you riding in my car.

(Chorus)

Spoken:
Well, my car has a windshield wiper for
  when it rains,
So make a wiper with your arm like this,
From side to side and go
Woosh, woosh, woosh!

I'm gonna send you home again,
I'm gonna send you home again,
I'm gonna send you home again,
Take you riding in my car.

(Chorus)

Body Part Movement March

ACTIVITY

1 Lead the class in clapping and counting to eight. Make sure everyone counts out loud and stops on the eighth count. Repeat several times.

2 Play the song "Body Part Movement March #1." Lead the class in performing the movements described in the song. Have volunteers take turns leading the class in the movements with the music.

3 Model different steady beat movements without the music, and have children practice the movements. Have children perform each movement eight times while counting aloud. Select from the lyric page, or create your own.

4 Have the class repeat this activity in time with "Body Part Movement March #2" (an instrumental version of the song). Make sure everyone counts to eight throughout the music.

EXTENSION

Have volunteers create and lead steady beat movements for the rest of the class to follow. Have the leaders practice doing their movements while counting to eight. Play "Body Part Movement March #2." Have the leaders take turns leading the class in the steady beat movement of their choice. Invite new leaders to repeat the activity.

Objectives

♪ To hear a steady beat in music

♪ To execute steady beat movements in groups of eight each

Skills

♪ Listening

♪ Coordination

♪ Counting

Music

CD #2, Tracks 16 and 17: "Body Part Movement March #1" and "Body Part Movement March #2"

Body Part Movement March

Words and Music by Steven Traugh
Copyright 1989, Kiducation (ASCAP)

Let's see if we can keep a steady beat together.
Let's count to eight and clap our hands eight times.
Ready, go!
1, 2, 3, 4, 5, 6, 7, 8
Clap your hands and count to eight.
1, 2, 3, 4, 5, 6, 7, 8
Pat your head eight times.
1, 2, 3, 4, 5, 6, 7, 8
Tap your eyebrows eight times.
1, 2, 3, 4, 5, 6, 7, 8
Pat your cheeks and smile.
1, 2, 3, 4, 5, 6, 7, 8
Tap your nose and alternate hands.
1, 2, 3, 4, 5, 6, 7, 8
Pat your chin and alternate hands.
1, 2, 3, 4, 5, 6, 7, 8
Tap your neck eight times.
1, 2, 3, 4, 5, 6, 7, 8
Pat your shoulders eight times.
1, 2, 3, 4, 5, 6, 7, 8
Lift weights eight times.
1, 2, 3, 4, 5, 6, 7, 8
Let's do that eight more times.
1, 2, 3, 4, 5, 6, 7, 8
Pat your stomach eight times.
1, 2, 3, 4, 5, 6, 7, 8
Lean back and pat your stomach.
1, 2, 3, 4, 5, 6, 7, 8
Tap your legs eight times.
1, 2, 3, 4, 5, 6, 7, 8
Tap your knees eight times.
1, 2, 3, 4, 5, 6, 7, 8

Hands on hips and knock your knees.
1, 2, 3, 4, 5, 6, 7, 8
Knock your knees eight more times.
1, 2, 3, 4, 5, 6, 7, 8
Flap your wings eight times.
1, 2, 3, 4, 5, 6, 7, 8
Flap your wings eight more times.
1, 2, 3, 4, 5, 6, 7, 8
Everybody jump eight times.
1, 2, 3, 4, 5, 6, 7, 8
Hop on one foot eight times.
1, 2, 3, 4, 5, 6, 7, 8
Hop on the other foot eight times.
1, 2, 3, 4, 5, 6, 7, 8
Do the twist eight times.
1, 2, 3, 4, 5, 6, 7, 8
Do the twist eight more times.
1, 2, 3, 4, 5, 6, 7, 8
Pat your bottom eight times.
1, 2, 3, 4, 5, 6, 7, 8
Do the twist and pat your bottom.
1, 2, 3, 4, 5, 6, 7, 8
Fingertips eight times.
1, 2, 3, 4, 5, 6, 7, 8
Tap your elbows eight times.
1, 2, 3, 4, 5, 6, 7, 8
Flap your wings and knock your knees.
1, 2, 3, 4, 5, 6, 7, 8
Flap your wings and knock your knees.
1, 2, 3, 4, 5, 6, 7, 8
Very nice job everybody!

Reading Rhythmic Notation #1

ACTIVITY

1 In advance, draw Example 1 (below) on a chalkboard or chart paper.

Example 1

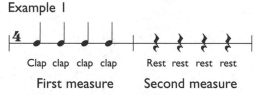

Clap clap clap clap   Rest rest rest rest

First measure   Second measure

2 Tell the class that the symbols in the first measure are one type of steady beat called *notes*. Have children clap on the beat whenever they see the note. Have children practice counting out loud to four while reading (clapping) the first measure of Example 1. Point to each note as the children count and clap.

3 Point to the symbols in the second measure, and explain that they are another type of steady beat called *rests*. Have children pause whenever they see a rest. Tell them a rest means they should not clap on that beat. Have children practice reading (clapping or resting) both measures. Point to each note or rest as children count slowly to four throughout each measure.

4 Tell children that you are now going to mix up both notes and rests. Add Example 2, and have the class practice clapping and resting. Point to each note or rest as the class counts slowly to four.

Example 2

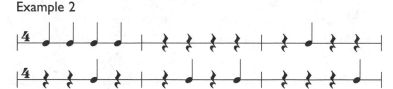

EXTENSION

Have volunteers use classroom rhythm instruments to perform Example 2 while the class claps the beat.

Objectives

♪ To learn to read quarter notes and rests as units of steady beats

♪ To perform rhythmic notation as a group

Skills

♪ Reading

♪ Rhythm

♪ Concentration

♪ Group Cooperation

Music

There is no music for this lesson.

28

Reading Rhythmic Notation #2

Objective

♪ To improve the skill of reading quarter notes and quarter rests

Skills

♪ Reading Rhythmic Notation

♪ Counting

♪ Rhythm

♪ Concentration

Music

CD #2, Track 17: "Body Part Movement March #2"

ACTIVITY

1 In advance, draw Example 1 on a chalkboard or chart paper.
Example 1

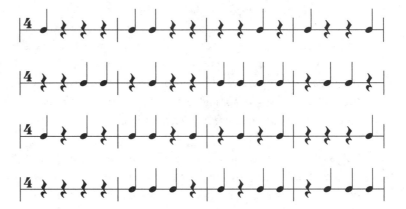

2 Review the names and functions of the quarter note and the quarter rest as previously discussed in Lesson 27. Have the class count 1, 2, 3, 4 with you as they read (clapping or resting) Example 1.

3 Go through the example slowly at first. Gradually pick up the tempo. Have volunteers clap the rhythm in front of the class.

EXTENSION

Lead the class in performing the notation from Example 1 in time with the song "Body Part Movement March #2."

The Hokey Pokey

ACTIVITY

1 Model the right side and the left side of your body for the class. Have them stand and imitate your movements. Because it is easier for young children to mirror your movements, stand in the front of the class and use your left side when they are to be using their right side and vice versa. Explain why you are switching sides.

2 Read each of the six verses in the song "The Hokey Pokey #1." Lead children in the movements described in the lyrics. Remember to use the opposite side indicated if your class is to mirror your movements.

3 Teach the class the following movements for the last three lines of each verse in the song:

You do the Hokey Pokey,   *(hands up, rock from side to side)*
And you turn yourself around. *(turn around, hands stay up)*
That's what it's all about.   *(clap hands on every syllable)*

4 Encourage them to sing the lyrics as they perform the movements they have learned.

5 Play "The Hokey Pokey #1." Lead the class in the movements called for in the lyrics. Repeat as desired.

6 Help the class create movements for the coda (last part) of the song. Play the song again, and have the class add these movements to the music.

EXTENSION

Play the song "The Hokey Pokey #2." Lead the class in the movements called for in the lyrics.

Objectives

♪ To learn left, right, and whole body movements

♪ To improve singing skills

Skills

♪ Recognition of Right and Left

♪ Movement

♪ Rhythmic Coordination

Music

CD #2, Tracks 18 and 19: "The Hokey Pokey #1" and "The Hokey Pokey #2"

The Hokey Pokey

Adapted by Greg Scelsa. Copyright 1985, Little House Music and Gregorian
Chance Music (ASCAP)

The Hokey Pokey #1

You put your right hand in.
You put your right hand out.
You put your right hand in,
And you shake it all about.
You do the Hokey Pokey,
And you turn yourself around.
That's what it's all about.

You put your left hand in.
You put your left hand out.
You put your left hand in,
And you shake it all about.
You do the Hokey Pokey,
And you turn yourself around.
That's what it's all about.

You put your right foot in.
Your right foot out.
Your right foot in,
And you shake it all about.
You do the Hokey Pokey,
And you turn yourself around.
That's what it's all about.

You put your left foot in.
Your left foot out.
Your left foot in,
And you shake it all about.
You do the Hokey Pokey,
And you turn yourself around.
That's what it's all about.

You put your head in.
Your head out.
Your head in,
And you shake it all about.
You do the Hokey Pokey,
And you turn yourself around.
That's what it's all about.

You put your whole self in.
Your whole self out.
Your whole self in,
And you shake it all about.
You do the Hokey Pokey,
And you turn yourself around.
That's what it's all about.

Coda:
    You do the Hokey Pokey.
    You do the Hokey Pokey.
    You do the Hokey Pokey.
    That's what it's all about.

The Hokey Pokey #2

right elbow
left elbow
right side
left side
knees
back side

Snowflake

ACTIVITY

1 In advance, get a coffee filter for each child. Show children how to fold their filter in half once and then again, so that the filter is in equal quarters. Next, show them how to use just the tips of their scissors to cut out small shapes in several places around the filter. Demonstrate using your own coffee filter. Write the lyrics to the song "Snowflake" on a chalkboard or chart paper to be displayed for the class.

2 Have children share their snowflake with the class.

3 Note how each snowflake is different from all the others.

4 Play "Snowflake," and track the words as the class listens to the song.

5 Have volunteers create and perform movements for each verse.

6 Have leaders perform the movements with the music. Encourage the class to sing along as they repeat the activity.

EXTENSION

Discuss the concept of strength through diversity. List the different kinds of occupations it takes to make the community work (e.g., teachers, law enforcement officers, farmers, doctors, scientists, custodians). Help children to see that, like snowflakes, we are all different and yet the same.

Objectives

♪ To improve singing skills

♪ To create movements to dramatize the lyrics of a song

♪ To explore the uniqueness of each individual

Skills

♪ Singing

♪ Creative Drama

♪ Reading

♪ Leadership

♪ Cooperation

Music

CD #2, Track 20: "Snowflake"

Snowflake

Words and Music by Greg Scelsa. Copyright 1995,
Gregorian Chance Music (ASCAP)

Did you know that you are the only one
In the world quite like you?
Did you know that there is no other one
Who can be that special you?

Chorus:
   We are all like a snowflake,
   Beautiful and unique.
   All we have to do is be ourselves
   And be the best we can be.

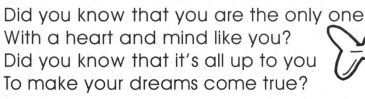

Did you know that you are the only one
With a heart and mind like you?
Did you know that it's all up to you
To make your dreams come true?

(Chorus)

Be yourself in all that you do,
To your heart you must be true.
Did you know we are all born with gifts
To nurture and to share?
Did you know when we look inside ourself
The more that we're aware, that…

(Chorus)

Be the best we can be.

Munchie Monster

Sunday	Monday	Tuesday	Wednesday	Thursday	Friday	Saturday

Monday—shortcake.   Tuesday—pie.   Wednesday—Popsicle.   Thursday—fries.   Friday—chocolate bar.   Saturday—cake.   Sunday—Ooh! A stomachache.